On the Farm

Poems Selected by Lee Bennett Hopkins

Illustrated by Laurel Molk

Little, Brown and Company
Boston Toronto London

For —
   M. Jean Greenlaw
      who
    sows
    poetry
      LBH

For Peter
LM

Compilation copyright © 1991 by Lee Bennett Hopkins
Illustrations copyright © 1991 by Laurel Molk

First Edition

Copyright acknowledgments appear on page 32.

Library of Congress Cataloging-in-Publication Data

On the farm / selected by Lee Bennett Hopkins ; illustrated by Laurel
  Molk. — 1st ed.
     p. cm.
    Poems.
    Summary: A collection of poems about farms and farm animals, by
    such authors as Aileen Fisher, David McCord, William Carlos
    Williams, and Myra Cohn Livingston.
    ISBN 0-316-37274-9
    1. Farm life — Juvenile poetry.   2. Children's poetry, American.
  [1. Farm life — Poetry.   2. American poetry — Collections.]
  I. Hopkins, Lee Bennett.   II. Molk, Laurel, ill.
  PS595.F3806   1991
  811.008′0321734 — dc20   90-6453

10 9 8 7 6 5 4 3 2 1

Published simultaneously in Canada
by Little, Brown & Company (Canada) Limited

Printed in Singapore

Contents

Hello, Farm

Hello, ducks,
chickens,
cows.

Hello, hen house,
stable,
barn.

Hello, woodpiles,
silo,
swing.

Hello,
hello,
everything.

Lee Bennett Hopkins

The Cow

The friendly cow all red and white,
    I love with all my heart:
She gives me cream with all her might,
    To eat with apple-tart.

She wanders lowing here and there,
    And yet she cannot stray,
All in the pleasant open air,
    The pleasant light of day;

And blown by all the winds that pass
    And wet with all the showers,
She walks among the meadow grass
    And eats the meadow flowers.

Robert Louis Stevenson

Foal

Come trotting up
Beside your mother,
Little skinny.

Lay your neck across
Her back, and whinny,
Little foal.

You think you're a horse
Because you can trot —
But you're not.

Your eyes are so wild,
And each leg is as tall
As a pole;

And you're only a skittish
Child, after all,
Little foal.

Mary Britton Miller

Familiar Friends

The horses, the pigs,
And the chickens,
The turkeys, the ducks
And the sheep!
I can see all my friends
From my window
As soon as I waken
From sleep.

The cat on the fence
Is out walking.
The geese have gone down
For a swim.
The pony comes trotting
Right up to the gate;
He knows I have candy
For him.

The cows in the pasture
Are switching
Their tails to keep off
The flies.
And the old mother dog
Has come out in the yard
With five pups to give me
A surprise.

James S. Tippett

Picking Berries

All day long
we picked and picked.

The sun was strong,
the bushes pricked.

The berries grew
in brambly places
where twigs untied
my sneaker laces.

We picked and picked
and picked some more.
The sun blazed down,
my arms got sore,

And then all night
as time went ticking
I dreamed I *still*
kept picking, picking.

Aileen Fisher

Lawnmower

The lawnmower
Grinds its teeth
Over the grass,
Spitting out a thick
Green spray;

Its head is too full
Of iron and oil
To know
What it throws
Away:

The lawn's whole
Crop of chopped
Soft,
Delicious
Green hay.

Valerie Worth

The Pickety Fence

The pickety fence
The pickety fence
Give it a lick it's
The pickety fence
Give it a lick it's
A clickety fence
Give it a lick it's
A lickety fence
Give it a lick
Give it a lick
Give it a lick
With a rickety stick
Pickety
Pickety
Pickety
Pick

David McCord

Country Window

Look at it rain
on the windowpane!

Look at it splash
from the roof's mustache!

Look at it pour
on the field's brown floor!

We stand and watch . . .
and nobody cares
if it rains and rains
on the garden chairs,
the road, the clover,
the grass, the wheat . . .

It's raining puddles
for wading feet.

Aileen Fisher

Pig

The pig is bigger
Than we had thought
And not so pink,
Fringed with white
Hairs that look
Gray, because while
They say a pig is clean,
It is not always; still,
We like this huge, cheerful,
Rich, soft-bellied beast —
It wants to be comfortable,
And does not care much
How the thing is managed.

Valerie Worth

At Grandpa's Farm

I went out to my grandpa's farm.
The billy goat filled me with alarm.

He chased me up an apple tree,
And clinging there I still would be,

If grandpa hadn't come that day
And chased the billy goat away.

Anonymous

The Rooster

Cock-a-doodle-doo!
    The rooster flaps his wings.
Cock-a-doodle-doo!
    He flaps his wings and sings.
Cock-a-doodle-doo!
    The rooster sings, and then
Cock-a-doodle!
Cock-a-doodle!
    He flaps his wings again.

Anonymous

The Red Wheelbarrow

so much depends
upon

a red wheel
barrow

glazed with rain
water

beside the white
chickens.

William Carlos Williams

October Morning

It's an apple-dumpling dandy day —
The gray mouse scampers through the hay,
Oak trees feel their crisp leaves curl,
Maples leap and twirl.

Now fields are singing songs to fall,
And earth pulls on October's shawl.
In every bush, birds shout "Hooray!"
This apple-dumpling dandy day.

Patricia Hubbell

Hay Song

The mower's in the meadow
scissoring grass,
tall tufted timothy
redtop and
rye,
                    (now let it lie)

felling alfalfa
clipping the clover,
bee, move over!
                    (let it dry)

scattering thistle
        in puffs
        of seed
smartweed
sneezeweed
daisy and
yarrow.

Pray
no rain tomorrow.
Let there be

hay,
meadow lunch
for a horse to munch
on a winter day.

Lilian Moore

Farmer

The farmer, worn from
long, field-days, trods home to a
welcome, warm supper.

Prince Redcloud

Prayer

Thank you for the sun,
      the sky,
    for all the things that like to fly,
      the shining rain that turns grass green,
      the earth we know —
      the world unseen —
for stars and night, and once again
      the every-morning sun. Amen.

Myra Cohn Livingston

Acknowledgments

Every effort has been made to trace the ownership of all copyrighted material and to secure the necessary permissions to reprint these selections. In the event of any question arising as to the use of any material, the editor and publisher, while expressing regret for any inadvertent error, will be happy to make the necessary correction in future printings.

Thanks are due for permission to reprint the following selections:

Atheneum Publishers, an imprint of Macmillan Publishing Company, for "October Morning" from *The Tigers Brought Pink Lemonade* by Patricia Hubbell. Copyright © 1988 by Patricia Hubbell; "Hay Song" from *Sam's Place* by Lilian Moore. Copyright © 1973 by Lilian Moore.

Curtis Brown Ltd. for "Hello, Farm" by Lee Bennett Hopkins. Copyright © 1991 by Lee Bennett Hopkins. By permission of Curtis Brown Ltd.

Farrar, Straus & Giroux, Inc., for "Pig" from *Small Poems* by Valerie Worth. Copyright © 1972 by Valerie Worth; "Lawnmower" from *More Small Poems* by Valerie Worth. Copyright © 1976 by Valerie Worth. Reprinted by permission of Farrar, Straus & Giroux, Inc.

HarperCollins Publishers for "Familiar Friends" from *Crickety Cricket!: The Best Loved Poems of James S. Tippett*. Originally appeared in *I Spend the Summer*. Copyright 1930 by James S. Tippett; renewed 1973 by Martha K. Tippett; "Picking Berries" and "Country Window" from *Out in the Dark and Daylight* by Aileen Fisher. Text copyright © 1980 by Aileen Fisher. All reprinted by permission of HarperCollins Publishers.

Little, Brown and Company for "The Pickety Fence" from *One at a Time* by David McCord. Copyright © 1952 by David McCord. By permission of Little, Brown and Company.

James N. Miller for "Foal" by Mary Britton Miller. Copyright estate of Mary Britton Miller.

New Directions Publishing Corporation for "The Red Wheelbarrow" from *Collected Poems, Volume I, 1909–1939* by William Carlos Williams. Copyright 1938 by New Directions Publishing Corporation. Reprinted by permission.

Prince Redcloud for "Farmer." Used by permission of the author, who controls all rights.

Marian Reiner for "Prayer" from *The Moon and a Star and Other Poems* by Myra Cohn Livingston. Copyright © 1965 by Myra Cohn Livingston. Reprinted by permission of Marian Reiner for the author.